KIDNEY DIET

Find out how to eat healthy and prevent kidney failure

ALICIA COLLIN

TABLE OF CONTANTS

Introduction

A kidney diet is a form of healthy eating that promotes kidney detoxification. Anyone can benefit from it, but it is especially recommended for those suffering from kidney failure.
In general, it includes a variety of foods in small amounts.
If you have chronic kidney disease and are following your doctor's instructions for treatment, it is important to follow these rules.

Here are some foundational principles:

- Drink plenty of water

When you drink water, it helps to keep your body hydrated by helping you absorb nutrients from food and waste products that you normally carry out through urine.

- Consume fish regularly

Fish is rich in long-chain omega-3 fatty acids, which are essential for a healthy heart and brain development in children. Infants and children may also be at risk of developing cases of rheumatoid arthritis, type 1 diabetes and other autoimmune diseases, asthma and allergies.

- Eat less protein

One should eat less protein to maintain a healthy diet. Protein is a necessary part of one's diet, but you should pay attention to how much protein is included in the form of food.
If you are working with your health care team, it may include dietary guidelines based on your physical needs.

If you are receiving dialysis treatment, it may be helpful to speak to a registered dietitian about making the appropriate adjustments for your individual needs.

- Take multivitamin, mineral, and vitamin D supplements

In addition to consuming plenty of fruits and vegetables in your daily diet, taking a multivitamin supplement may also help boost your overall nutrition. Speak to your doctor about which type of vitamin supplements would be appropriate for you.

- Choose complex carbohydrates over simple carbohydrates

Complex carbohydrates are slowly digested, while simple carbohydrates are quickly digested and converted to simple sugar so they should be eaten in moderation.

- Choose fruits that are rich in antioxidants

There are two main types of antioxidants: vitamin A and vitamin C. Both vitamins fight free radicals, which have been linked to chronic diseases such as cancer, heart disease and diabetes. Eating fruits that are high in vitamin A may help reduce your risk of developing some types of cancers, but increases the risk of other types of cancers.

- Consume foods that are low in saturated fat

Saturated fat is found primarily in fatty cuts of meat that contain cholesterol. Eating fatty meat can increase the risk of chronic diseases like heart disease and diabetes, so your body should be provided with healthy sources of fat to replace it. The ideal type is omega 3 fatty acids, which are found naturally in fish and plant sources.

Stay well hydrated by drinking at least eight glasses of fluids per day and taking any special medications or supplements that have been prescribed by your doctor according to the instructions given to you.

- Consume ample amounts of foods that are rich in fiber and soluble fiber

Soluble fiber can help lower blood cholesterol levels. Your diet should include at least 17 grams of soluble fiber per day.

- Drink plenty of fluids

Keep your body well hydrated by drinking at least eight glasses of fluids per day and taking any special medications or supplements that have been prescribed by your doctor according to the instructions given to you.

- Eat six times a day

Eat at regular intervals. Eating small meals throughout the day will help prevent your body from going longer than three hours without food.

- Choose foods that are rich in antioxidants

There are two main types of antioxidants: vitamin A and vitamin C. Both vitamins fight free radicals, which have been linked to chronic diseases such as cancer, heart disease and diabetes. Eating fruits that are high in vitamin A may help reduce your risk of developing some types of cancers, but increases the risk of other types of cancers.

- Consume plenty of green, leafy vegetables

Green, leafy vegetables such as broccoli, brussels sprouts and cabbage are high in vitamins and minerals. Your diet should include at least three meals a week that include at least one serving of these types of vegetables.

- Consume foods that are high in antioxidants such as vitamin A and vitamin C

There are two main types of antioxidants: vitamin A and vitamin C. Both vitamins fight free radicals, which have been linked to chronic diseases such as cancer, heart disease and diabetes.

This cookbook ensures that you will be able to cook for yourself so you can maintain optimal health even if you are on a renal diet.

Breakfast

French Toast with Applesauce

Preparation Time: 5 minutes

Cooking Time: 15 minutes

Servings: 6

Ingredients:

- ¼ cup unsweetened applesauce
- ½ cup almond milk
- 1 teaspoon ground cinnamon
- 2 eggs
- 2 tablespoons white sugar

Directions:

1. Mix well applesauce, sugar, cinnamon, almond milk and eggs in a mixing bowl.
2. Soak the bread, one by one into applesauce mixture until wet.
3. On medium fire, heat a nonstick skillet greased with cooking spray.
4. Add soaked bread one at a time and cook for 2-3 minutes per side or until lightly browned.
5. Serve and enjoy.

Nutrition: Calories: 57; Carbs: 6g; Protein: 4g; Fats: 4g; Phosphorus: 69mg; Potassium: 88mg; Sodium: 43mg

Turkey and Spinach Scramble On Melba Toast

Preparation Time: 5 minutes

Cooking Time: 15 minutes

Servings: 2

Ingredients:

- 1 tsp. Extra virgin olive oil
- 1 cup Raw spinach
- ½ clove, minced Garlic
- 1 tsp. grated Nutmeg
- 1 cup Cooked and diced turkey breast
- 4 slices Melba toast
- 1 tsp. Balsamic vinegar

Directions:

1. Heat a skillet over medium heat and add oil.
2. Add turkey and heat through for 6 to 8 minutes.
3. Add spinach, garlic, and nutmeg and stir-fry for 6 minutes more.
4. Plate up the Melba toast and top with spinach and turkey scramble.
5. Drizzle with balsamic vinegar and serve.

Nutrition: Calories: 301 Fat: 19g Carb: 12g Protein: 19g Sodium: 360mg Potassium: 269mg Phosphorus: 215mg

Cheesy Scrambled Eggs with Fresh Herbs

Preparation Time: 15 minutes

Cooking Time: 10 minutes

Servings: 4

Ingredients:

- 3 Eggs
- 2 Egg whites
- ½ cup Cream cheese
- ¼ cup Unsweetened rice milk
- 1 tbsp. green part only Chopped scallion
- 1 tbsp. Chopped fresh tarragon
- 2 tbsps. Unsalted butter
- Ground black pepper to taste

Directions:

1. Whisk the eggs, egg whites, cream cheese, rice milk, scallions, and tarragon. Mix until smooth.
2. Melt the butter in a skillet.
3. Put egg mixture and cook for 5 minutes or until the eggs are thick and curds creamy.
4. Season with pepper and serve.

Nutrition: Calories: 221 Fat: 19g Carb: 3g Protein: 8g Sodium: 193mg Potassium: 140mg Phosphorus: 119mg

Buckwheat and Grapefruit Porridge

Preparation Time: 5 minutes

Cooking Time: 20 minutes

Servings: 2

Ingredients:

- ½ cup Buckwheat
- ¼ chopped Grapefruit
- 1 Tbsp. Honey
- 1 ½ cups Almond milk
- 2 cups Water

Directions:

1. Let the water boil on the stove. Add the buckwheat and place the lid on the pan.
2. Lower heat slightly and simmer for 7 to 10 minutes, checking to ensure water does not dry out.
3. When most of the water is absorbed, remove, and set aside for 5 minutes.
4. Drain any excess water from the pan and stir in almond milk, heating through for 5 minutes.
5. Add the honey and grapefruit.
6. Serve.

Nutrition: Calories: 231 Fat: 4g Carb: 43g Protein: 13g Sodium: 135mg Potassium: 370mg Phosphorus: 165mg

Lunch

Easy Lettuce Wraps

Preparation Time: 15 minutes

Cooking Time: 0 minutes

Servings: 4

Ingredients:

- 8 ounces cooked chicken, shredded
- 1 scallion, chopped
- ½ cup seedless red grapes, halved
- 1 celery stalk, chopped
- ¼ cup mayonnaise
- A pinch ground black pepper
- 4 large lettuce leaves

Directions:

1. In a mixing bowl add the scallion, chicken, celery, grapes and mayonnaise.
2. Stir well until incorporated.
3. Season with pepper.
4. Place the lettuce leaves onto serving plates.
5. Place the chicken salad onto the leaves.
6. Serve and enjoy!

Nutrition: Calories 146 Fat 5 g Cholesterol 35 mg Carbohydrates 8 g Sugar 4 g Fiber 0 g Protein 16 g Sodium 58 mg Calcium 18 mg Phosphorus 125 mg Potassium 212 mg

Fish Taco Filling

Preparation Time: 15 minutes

Cooking Time: 10 minutes

Servings: 4

Ingredients:

- 2 tablespoons extra-virgin olive oil
- 2 shallots, minced
- 3 (6-ounce) sole fillets, cut into strips
- 2 teaspoons chili powder
- 1 lime, zested and juiced
- 3 cups cabbage coleslaw mix with carrots

Directions:

1. In a large skillet, heat the olive oil over medium heat.
2. Add the shallots and cook for 3 minutes, stirring, until softened.
3. Add the sole fillets and sprinkle with the chili powder. Cook for 3 to 5 minutes, stirring gently, until the fish flakes when tested with a fork. Remove the skillet from the heat.
4. Drizzle the lime zest and juice over the fish.
5. Serve with the coleslaw in tacos or over rice.
6. Increase Protein Tip: To make this a medium-protein recipe, add one more 6-ounce sole fillet. The protein content will increase to 18g per serving.

7. Ingredient Tip: If you like spicy food, you can add 1 diced medium jalapeño pepper to the shallots or add ½ teaspoon of red pepper flakes to the fish mixture along with the lime juice and zest.

Nutrition: Calories: 176; Total fat: 9g; Saturated fat: 1g; Sodium: 315mg; Phosphorus: 265mg; Potassium: 451mg; Carbohydrates: 14g; Fiber: 4g; Protein: 13g; Sugar: 6g

Peanut Butter and Jelly Grilled Sandwich

Preparation Time: 5 minutes

Cooking Time: 5 minutes

Servings: 1

Ingredients:

- 2 tsp. butter (unsalted)
- 6 tsp. butter (peanut)
- 3 tsp. of flavored jelly
- 2 pieces of bread

Directions:

1. Put the peanut butter evenly on one bread. Add the layer of jelly.
2. Butter the outside of the pieces of bread.
3. Add the sandwich to a frying pan and toast both sides.

Nutrition: Calories: 300 Fat: 7g Carbs: 49g Protein: 8g Sodium: 460mg Potassium: 222mg Phosphorus: 80mg

Roasted Cod with Plums

Preparation Time: 10 minutes

Cooking Time: 20 minutes

Servings: 4

Ingredients:

- 6 red plums, halved and pitted
- 1½ pounds cod fillets
- 3 tablespoons extra-virgin olive oil
- 2 tablespoons freshly squeezed lemon juice
- ½ teaspoon dried thyme leaves
- 1/8 teaspoon salt
- 1/8 teaspoon freshly ground black pepper
- ¾ cup plain whole-almond milk yogurt, for serving

Directions:

1. Preheat the oven to 375°F. Line a baking sheet with parchment paper.
2. Arrange the plums, cut-side up, along with the fish on the prepared baking sheet. Drizzle with the olive oil and lemon juice and sprinkle with the thyme, salt, and pepper.
3. Roast for 15 to 20 minutes or until the fish flakes when tested with a fork and the plums are tender.
4. Serve with the yogurt.
5. Ingredient Tip: There's no need to measure out exactly 2 tablespoons of lemon juice. A standard-size lemon

has approximately 2 tablespoons juice in it. Simply squeeze all the juice from the lemon, being careful to avoid squeezing in the seeds.

Nutrition: Calories: 230; Total fat: 9g; Saturated fat: 2g; Sodium: 154mg; Phosphorus: 197mg; Potassium: 437mg; Carbohydrates: 10g; Fiber: 1g; Protein: 27g; Sugar: 8g

Corn and Shrimp Quiche

Preparation Time: 15 minutes

Cooking Time: 50 minutes

Servings: 6

Ingredients:

- 1 cup small cooked shrimp
- 1½ cups frozen corn, thawed and drained
- 5 large eggs, beaten
- 1 cup unsweetened almond milk
- Pinch salt
- 1/8 teaspoon freshly ground black pepper

Directions:

1. Preheat the oven to 350°F. Spray a 9-inch pie pan with nonstick baking spray.
2. In the prepared pan, combine the shrimp and corn.
3. In a medium bowl, beat the eggs, almond milk, salt, and pepper. Gently pour into the pan.
4. Bake for 45 to 55 minutes or until the quiche is puffed, set to the touch, and light golden brown on top. Let stand for 10 minutes before cutting into wedges to serve.
5. Ingredient Tip: Shrimp are measured according to the number per pound. So bigger shrimp have a lower number per pound. For this recipe, small shrimp should be about 50 per pound. Medium shrimp are

usually 36 to 40 per pound. You can cut larger shrimp into small pieces instead of buying small shrimp if you'd like.

Nutrition: Calories: 198; Total fat: 10g; Saturated fat: 4g; Sodium: 238mg; Phosphorus: 260mg; Potassium: 261mg; Carbohydrates: 9g; Fiber: 1g; Protein: 20g; Sugar: 2g

Dinner

Creamy Chicken with Cider

Preparation Time: 25 minutes

Cooking Time: 20 minutes

Servings: 4

Ingredients:

- 4 bone-in chicken breasts
- 2 tbsp. of lightly salted butter
- ¾ cup of apple cider vinegar
- 2/3 cup of rich unsweetened coconut almond milk or cream
- Kosher pepper

Directions:

1. Melt the butter in a skillet over medium heat.
2. Season the chicken with the pepper and add to the skillet. Cook over low heat for approx. 20 minutes.
3. Remove the chicken from the heat and set aside in a dish.
4. In the same skillet, add the cider and bring to a boil until most of it has evaporated.
5. Add the coconut cream and let cook for 1 minute until slightly thickened.
6. Pour the cider cream over the cooked chicken and serve.

Nutrition: Calories: 86.76kcal Carbohydrate: 1.88g Protein: 1.5g Sodium: 93.52mg Potassium: 74.65mg Phosphorus: 36.54mg Dietary Fiber: 0.1g Fat: 8.21g

Golden Eggplant Fries

Preparation Time: 10 minutes

Cooking Time: 15 minutes

Servings: 8

Ingredients:

- 2 eggs
- 2 cups almond flour
- 2 tablespoons coconut oil, spray
- 2 eggplants, peeled and cut thinly
- Sunflower seeds and pepper

Directions:

1. Preheat your oven to 400 degrees F.
2. Take a bowl and mix with sunflower seeds and black pepper.
3. Take another bowl and beat eggs until frothy.
4. Dip the eggplant pieces into the eggs.
5. Then coat them with the flour mixture.
6. Add another layer of flour and egg.
7. Then, take a baking sheet and grease with coconut oil on top.
8. Bake for about 15 minutes.
9. Serve and enjoy!

Nutrition: Calories: 212 Fat: 15.8g Carbohydrates: 12.1g Protein: 8.6g Phosphorus: 150mg Potassium: 147mg Sodium: 105mg

Chicken Fajitas

Preparation Time: 10 minutes

Cooking Time: 10 minutes

Servings: 8

Ingredients:

- 8 flour tortillas, 6" size
- 1/4 cup green pepper, cut in strips
- 1/4 cup red pepper, cut in strips
- 1/2 cup onion, sliced
- 1/2 cup cilantro
- 2 tbsp. canola oil
- 12 oz. boneless chicken breasts
- 1/4 tsp. black pepper
- 2 tsp. chili powder
- 1/2 tsp. cumin
- 2 tbsp. lemon juice

Directions:

1. Start by wrapping the tortillas in a foil.
2. Warm them up for 10 minutes in a preheated oven at 300 degrees f.
3. Add oil to a nonstick pan.
4. Add lemon juice chicken and seasoning
5. Stir fry for 5 minutes then add onion and peppers.
6. Continue cooking for 5 minutes or until chicken is tender.

7. Stir in cilantro, mix well and serve in tortillas.

Nutrition: Calories: 343 kcal Total Fat: 13 g Saturated Fat: 0 g Cholesterol: 53 mg Sodium: 281 mg Total Carbs: 33 g

Sirloin with Squash and Pineapple

Preparation Time: 10 minutes

Cooking Time: 9 minutes

Servings: 2

Ingredients:

- 8 ounces canned pineapple slices
- 2 garlic cloves, minced
- 2 teaspoons ginger root, minced
- 3 teaspoons olive oil
- 1-pound sirloin tips
- 1 medium zucchini, diced
- 1 medium yellow squash, diced
- 1/2 medium red onion, diced

Directions:

1. Mix pineapple juice with 1 teaspoon olive oil, ginger, and garlic in a Ziplock bag.
2. Add sirloin tips to the pineapple juice marinade and seal the bag.
3. Place the bag in the refrigerator overnight.
4. Preheat oven to 450ºF.
5. Layer 2 sheet pans with foil and grease it with 1 teaspoon olive oil.
6. Spread the squash, onion, and pineapple rings in the prepared pans.

7. Bake them for 5 minutes then transfer to the serving plate.
8. Place the marinated sirloin tips on a baking sheet and bake for 4 minutes in the oven.
9. Transfer the sirloin tips to the roasted vegetables.
10. Serve.

Nutrition: Calories: 264 kcal Total Fat: 12 g Saturated Fat: 0 g Cholesterol: 74 mg Sodium: 150 mg Total Carbs: 14 g

Beef Bulgogi

Preparation Time: 10 minutes

Cooking Time: 5 minutes

Servings: 4

Ingredients:

- 1-pound flank steak, thinly sliced
- 5 tablespoons Worcestershire sauce
- 2 1/2 tablespoons honey
- 1/4 cup chopped green onion
- 2 tablespoons minced garlic
- 2 tablespoons olive oil
- 1/2 teaspoon ground black pepper

Directions:

1. Place the beef in a shallow dish. Combine Worcestershire sauce, honey, green onion, garlic, olive oil, and ground black pepper in a small bowl. Pour over beef. Cover and refrigerate for at least 1 hour or overnight.
2. Preheat an outdoor grill for high heat, and lightly oil the grate.
3. Quickly grill beef on hot grill until slightly charred and cooked through, 1 to 2 minutes per side

Nutrition: Calories 348, Total Fat 16.5g, Saturated Fat 4.9g, Cholesterol 62mg, Sodium 272mg, Total Carbohydrate 16.6g, Dietary Fiber 0.4g, Total Sugar 14.7g,

Snacks

Lemon-Pepper Cucumbers

Preparation time: 5 minutes

Cooking time: 0 minutes

Servings: 2

Ingredients:

- 1 large cucumber, sliced
- Lemon juice, to taste
- Freshly ground pepper to taste

Directions:

1. Place cucumber slices on a serving platter. Trickle lemon juice over it. Garnish with pepper and serve.

Nutrition: calories 24 fat 0 g Carbohydrate 6 g Protein 1 g

Falafel

Preparation time: 30 minutes

Cooking time: 15 minutes

Servings: 2

Ingredients:

- 1 cup dried chickpeas (do not use cooked or canned)
- ½ cup fresh parsley leaves, discard stems
- ¼ cup fresh dill leaves, discard stems
- ½ cup fresh cilantro leaves
- 4 cloves garlic, peeled
- ½ tablespoon ground black pepper
- ½ tablespoon ground coriander
- ½ tablespoon ground cumin
- ½ teaspoon cayenne pepper (optional)
- ½ teaspoon baking powder
- ¼ teaspoon baking soda
- Salt to taste
- 1 tablespoon toasted sesame seeds
- Oil, as required

Directions:

1. Rinse chickpeas and soak in water overnight. Cover with at least 3 inches of water. Drain and dry by patting with a kitchen towel.

2. Add all the fresh herbs into a food processor. Process until finely chopped. Add chickpeas, spices and garlic

and pulse for not more than 40 seconds each time until smooth.

3. Transfer into a container. Cover and chill for at least 1 hour or until use. Divide the mixture into 12 equal portions and shape into patties.
4. Place a deep pan over medium heat. Pour enough oil to cover at least 3 inches from the bottom of the pan.
5. When the oil is well heated, but not smoking, drop falafel, a few at a time and fry until medium brown.
6. Remove with a spoon and place on a plate lined with paper towels. Serve with a dip of your choice.

Nutrition: calories 93 fat 3.8 g carbohydrate 1.3 g Protein 3.9 g

Walnut-Feta Yogurt Dip

Preparation time: 15 minutes + chilling

Cooking time: 0 minutes

Servings: 8 (2 tablespoons dip without vegetable sticks)

Ingredients:

- 2 cups plain low-fat yogurt
- ¼ cup crumbled feta cheese
- 3 tablespoons chopped walnuts or pine nuts
- 1 teaspoon chopped fresh oregano or marjoram or ½ teaspoon dried oregano or marjoram, crushed
- Freshly ground pepper to taste
- Salt to taste
- 1 tablespoon snipped dried tomatoes (not oil packed)
- Salt to taste
- Walnut halves to garnish
- Assorted vegetable sticks to serve

Directions:

1. For yogurt dip, place 3 layers of cotton cheesecloth over a strainer. Place strainer over a bowl. Add yogurt into the strainer. Cover the strainer with cling wrap. Refrigerate for 24-48 hours.
2. Discard the strained liquid and add yogurt into a bowl. Add feta cheese, walnuts, seasoning, and herbs and mix well. Cover and chill for an hour.

3. Garnish with walnut halves. Serve with vegetable sticks.

Nutrition: Calories 68 Fat 4 g Carbohydrate 5 g Protein 4 g

Date Wraps

Preparation time: 10 minutes

Cooking time: 0 minutes

Servings: 8

Ingredients:

- 8 whole dates, pitted
- 8 thin slices prosciutto
- Freshly ground pepper to taste

Directions:

1. Take one date and one slice prosciutto. Wrap the prosciutto around the dates and place on a serving platter. Garnish with pepper and serve.

Nutrition: calories 35 fat 1 g Carbohydrate 6 g Protein 2 g

Clementine & Pistachio Ricotta

Preparation time: 5 minutes

Cooking time: 0 minutes

Servings: 2

Ingredients:

- 2/3 cup part-skim ricotta
- 2 clementine's, peeled, separated into segments, deseeded
- 4 teaspoons chopped pistachio nuts

Directions:

1. Place 1/3 cup ricotta in each of 2 bowls. Divide the clementine segments equally and place over the ricotta. Sprinkle pistachio nuts on top and serve.

Nutrition: calories 178 fat 9 g carbohydrate 15 g Protein 11 g

Serrano-Wrapped Plums

Preparation time: 10 minutes

Cooking time: 0 minutes

Servings: 4

Ingredients:

- 2 firm ripe plums or peaches or nectarines, quartered
- 1 ounce thinly sliced serrano ham or prosciutto or jamón ibérico, cut into 8 pieces

Directions:

1. Take one piece of ham and one piece of fruit. Wrap the ham around the fruit and place on a serving platter. Serve.

Nutrition: calories 30 fat 1 g Carbohydrate 4 g Protein 2 g

Greek Salad Wraps

Preparation Time: 15 minutes

Cooking Time: 10 minutes

Servings: 2

Ingredients:

- 1½ cups seedless cucumber, peeled and chopped (about 1 large cucumber)
- 1 cup chopped tomato (about 1 large tomato)
- ½ cup finely chopped fresh mint
- 1 (2.25-ounce) can sliced black olives (about ½ cup), drained
- ¼ cup diced red onion (about ¼ onion)
- 2 tablespoons extra-virgin olive oil
- 1 tablespoon red wine vinegar
- ¼ teaspoon freshly ground black pepper
- ¼ teaspoon kosher or sea salt
- ½ cup crumbled goat cheese (about 2 ounces)
- 4 whole-wheat flatbread wraps or soft whole-wheat tortillas

Directions:

1. In a large bowl, mix together the cucumber, tomato, mint, olives, and onion until well combined.
2. In a small bowl, whisk together the oil, vinegar, pepper, and salt. Drizzle the dressing over the salad, and mix gently.

3. With a knife, spread the goat cheese evenly over the four wraps. Spoon a quarter of the salad filling down the middle of each wrap.

4. Fold up each wrap: start by folding up the bottom, then fold one side over and fold the other side over the top. Repeat with the remaining wraps and serve.

Nutrition: calories: 262; total fat: 15g; saturated fat: 5g; cholesterol: 15mg; sodium: 529mg; total carbohydrates: 23g; fiber: 4g; protein: 7g

Baked Veggie Turmeric Nuggets

Preparation Time: 10 minutes

Cooking Time: 25 minutes

Servings: 24

Ingredients:

- 2 cups Broccoli florets
- ¼ tsp. Sea salt
- 2 cups Cauliflower florets
- 1 tsp. Minced garlic
- ½ cup Almond meal
- 1 cup Chopped carrots
- ½ tsp. Turmeric powder
- 1 large Whole egg
- ¼ tsp. Black pepper powder

Directions:

1. Prep oven by preheating to 400°F.
2. Get a parchment-lined baking sheet ready.
3. Pour cauliflower, turmeric, broccoli, carrots, black pepper, garlic, and sea salt in the blender and blitz until it's smooth.
4. Pour in the egg and almond meal and mix until it's incorporated.
5. Pour the paste into a mixing bowl. Scoop out a bit onto your hand and form a circular disc. Place this disc on

the baking sheet and repeat the process until the mixing bowl is empty.

6. Slide into the oven then bake for at least 15 minutes on one before flipping and baking for 10 minutes on the other side.

7. Serve with a side of Paleo ranch sauce.

Nutrition: Calories: 12 kcal Protein: 0.88 g Fat: 0.52 g Carbohydrates: 1.12 g

Ginger Flour Banana Ginger Bars

Preparation Time: 10 minutes

Cooking Time: 40 minutes

Servings: 4-6

Ingredients:

- 1 cup Coconut flour
- 1 ½ tbsp. Grated ginger
- 2 large ripe apple
- 1 tsp. Baking soda
- 1/3 cup melted butter
- 2 tsp. Cinnamon
- 2 tsp. Apple cider vinegar
- 1/3 cup Honey or maple syrup
- 1 tsp. Ground cardamom
- media While eggs

Directions:

1. Prep the oven by preheating to 350ºF.
2. Line a glass baking dish with parchment paper. If you don't have any paper, just grease the pan.
3. Put all the ingredients except the baking soda and apple cider vinegar through a food processor and blend until it's all mixed up.
4. Now add the last two ingredients and blitz once before pouring the mix into the glass dish.

5. Bake up to a toothpick inserted into the center comes out clean. This usually takes 40 minutes.

Nutrition: Calories: 1407 kcal Protein: 42.18 g Fat: 100.26 g Carbohydrates: 88.33 g

Turmeric Coconut Flour Muffins

Preparation Time: 5 minutes

Cooking Time: 25 minutes

Servings: 8

Ingredients:

- ½ cup unsweetened coconut almond milk
- ¾ cup & 2 tbsp. Coconut flour
- 1 tsp. Vanilla extract
- large Whole eggs
- ½ tsp. Baking soda
- 1/3 cup Maple syrup
- 2 tsp. Turmeric
- Pepper and salt
- ½ tsp. Ginger powder

Directions:

1. Prep oven by preheating to 350ºF.
2. Line 8 muffin tins with 8 muffin liners.
3. Whisk eggs, maple syrup, almond milk, and vanilla extract in a mixing bowl until the egg starts to form bubbles.
4. In a different bowl, mix the coconut flour, turmeric powder, pepper, baking soda, ginger powder, and salt.
5. Put the dry mixture into the wet mixture then stir until it's all mixed and thick.
6. Spoon out the batter into prepared muffin tins.

7. Leave to bake for 25 minutes or until it looked golden.
8. Let the muffins cool for 1-2 minutes before transferring them to a rack.

Nutrition: Calories: 143 kcal Protein: 6.18 g Fat: 8 g Carbohydrates: 11.8 g

Tangy Turmeric Flavored Florets

Preparation Time: 10 minutes

Cooking Time: 55 minutes

Servings: 1

Ingredients:

- 1-head cauliflower, chopped into florets
- 1-Tbsp olive oil
- 1-Tbsp turmeric
- A pinch of cumin
- A dash of salt

Directions:

1. Set the oven to 400°F.
2. Put all together the ingredients in a baking pan. Mix well until thoroughly combined.
3. Cover the pan with foil. Roast for 40 minutes. Remove the foil cover and roast additionally for 15 minutes.

Nutrition: Calories: 90 Fat: 3g Protein: 4.5g Sodium: 87mg

Total Carbs: 16.2g Dietary Fiber: 5g Net Carbs: 11.2g

Cereal Chia Chips

Preparation Time: 10 minutes

Cooking Time: 30 minutes

Servings: 10

Ingredients:

- ¼-cup rolled oats, gluten-free
- ½-cup white quinoa, uncooked
- ¾-cup pecans, chopped
- 2-Tbsps chia seeds
- 2-Tbsps coconut sugar
- A pinch of sea salt (optional)
- 2-Tbsps coconut oil
- ½-cup maple syrup

Directions:

1. Preheat your oven to 325°F. Line a baking pan with parchment paper.
2. Stir in the first six ingredients in a mixing bowl. Mix well until thoroughly combined. Set aside.
3. Pour the oil and syrup in a small saucepan placed over medium-low heat. Heat the mixture for 3 minutes, stirring occasionally.
4. Fold in the dry ingredients; stir well to coat thoroughly.
5. Pour the mixture in the baking pan, and spread to an even layer using a spoon.

6. Put the pan in the oven. Bake for 15 minutes. Turn the pan around to cook evenly. Bake for 8-10 minutes until the mixture turns golden brown.

7. Allow cooling entirely before breaking the chips into bite-size pieces.

Nutrition: Calories: 157 Fat: 5.2g Protein: 7.8g S Sodium: 25mg Total Carbs: 22.1g Dietary Fiber: 2.5g Net Carbs: 19.6g

Sweet Savory Meatballs

Preparation time: 10 minutes

Cooking time: 20 minutes

Servings: 12

Ingredients

- 1-pound ground turkey
- 1 large egg
- 1/4 cup bread crumbs
- 2 tablespoon onion, finely chopped
- 1 teaspoon garlic powder
- 1/2 teaspoon black pepper
- 1/4 cup canola oil
- 6-ounce grape jelly
- 1/4 cup chili sauce

Directions

1. Place all ingredients except chili sauce and jelly in a large mixing bowl.
2. Mix well until evenly mixed then make small balls out of this mixture.
3. It will make about 48 meatballs. Spread them out on a greased pan on a stovetop.
4. Cook them over medium heat until brown on all the sides.
5. Mix chili sauce with jelly in a microwave-safe bowl and heat it for 2 minutes in the microwave.

6. Pour this chili sauce mixture onto the meatballs in the pan.
7. Transfer the meatballs in the pan to the preheated oven.
8. Bake the meatballs for 20 minutes in an oven at 375 degrees f.
9. Serve fresh and warm.

Nutrition: calories 127. Protein 9 g. Carbohydrates 14 g. Fat 4 g. Cholesterol 41 mg. Sodium 129 mg. Potassium 148 mg. Phosphorus 89 mg. Calcium 15 mg. Fiber 0.2 g.

Mixes of Snack

Preparation time: 10 minutes

Cooking time: 1 hours and 15 minutes

Servings: 4

Ingredients

- 6 cup margarine
- 2 tablespoon Worcestershire sauce
- 1 ½ tablespoon spice salt
- ¾ cup garlic powder
- ½ teaspoon onion powder
- 3 cups crispy
- 3 cups cheerios
- 3 cups corn flakes
- 1 cup kite
- 1 cup pretzels
- 1 cup broken bagel chips into 1-inch pieces

Directions

1. Preheat the oven to 250f (120c)
2. Melt the margarine in a pan. Stir in the seasoning. Gradually add the ingredients remaining by mixing so that the coating is uniform.
3. Cook 1 hour, stirring every 15 minutes. Spread on paper towels to let cool. Store in a tightly-closed container.

Nutrition: calories: 200 kcal total fat: 9 g saturated fat: 3.5 g cholesterol: 0 mg   sodium: 3.5 mg total carbs: 27 g fiber: 2 g sugar: 0 g   protein: 3 g

Chicken Pepper Bacon Wraps

Preparation time: 10 minutes

Cooking time: 15 minutes

Servings: 4

Ingredients

- 1 medium onion, chopped
- 12 strips bacon, halved
- 12 fresh jalapenos peppers
- 12 fresh banana peppers
- 2 pounds boneless, skinless chicken breast

Directions

1. How to prepare:
2. Grease a grill rack with cooking spray and preheat the grill on low heat.
3. Slice the peppers in half lengthwise then remove their seeds.
4. Dice the chicken into small pieces and divide them into each pepper.
5. Now spread the chopped onion over the chicken in the peppers.
6. Wrap the bacon strips around the stuffed peppers.
7. Place these wrapped peppers in the grill and cook them for 15 minutes.
8. Serve fresh and warm.

Nutrition: calories 71. Protein 10 g. Carbohydrates 1 g. Fat 3 g. Cholesterol 26 mg. Sodium 96 mg. Potassium 147 mg. Phosphorus 84 mg. Calcium 9 mg. Fiber 0.8 g.

Side dishes

Cauliflower Patties

Preparation Time: 5 minutes

Cooking Time: 8 minutes

Servings: 4

Ingredients:

- Eggs – 2
- Egg whites – 2
- Onion – ½, diced
- Cauliflower – 2 cups, frozen
- All-purpose white flour – 2 Tbsps.
- Black pepper – 1 tsp.
- Coconut oil – 1 Tbsp.
- Curry powder – 1 tsp.
- Fresh cilantro – 1 Tbsp.

Directions:

1. Soak vegetables in warm water before cooking.
2. Steam cauliflower over a pan of boiling water for 10 minutes.
3. Blend eggs and onion in a food processor before adding cooked cauliflower, spices, cilantro, flour, and pepper and blast in the processor for 30 seconds.
4. Heat a skillet on a high heat and add oil.
5. Enjoy with a salad.

Nutrition: Calories: 227 Fat: 12g Carb: 15g Phosphorus: 193mg

Potassium: 513mg Sodium: 158mg Protein: 13g

Kale Chips

Preparation Time: 20 minutes

Cooking Time: 25 minutes

Servings: 6

Ingredients:

- Kale – 2 cups
- Olive oil – 2 tsp.
- Chili powder – ¼ tsp.
- Pinch cayenne pepper

Directions:

1. Preheat the oven to 300F.
2. Line 2 baking sheets with parchment paper; set aside.
3. Remove the stems from the kale and tear the leaves into 2-inch pieces.
4. Wash the kale and dry it completely.
5. Handover the kale to a large bowl and drizzle with olive oil.
6. Use your hands to toss the kale with oil, taking care to coat each leaf evenly.
7. Season the kale with chili powder and cayenne pepper and toss to combine thoroughly.
8. Spread the seasoned kale in a single layer on each baking sheet. Do not overlap the leaves.
9. Bake the kale, rotating the pans once, for 20 to 25 minutes until it is crisp and dry.

10. Take out the oven trays and allow the chips to cool on the trays for 5 minutes.
11. Serve.

Nutrition: Calories: 24 Fat: 2g Carb: 2g Phosphorus: 21mg Potassium: 111mg Sodium: 13mg Protein: 1g

Turnip Chips

Preparation Time: 5 minutes

Cooking Time: 50 minutes

Servings: 2

Ingredients:

- Turnips – 2, peeled and sliced
- Extra virgin olive oil – 1 Tbsp.
- Onion – 1 chopped
- Minced garlic – 1 clove
- Black pepper – 1 tsp.
- Oregano – 1 tsp.
- Paprika - 1 1 tsp.

Directions:

1. Preheat oven to 375F. Grease a baking tray with olive oil.
2. Add turnip slices in a thin layer.
3. Dust over herbs and spices with an extra drizzle of olive oil.
4. Bake 40 minutes. Turning once.

Nutrition: Calories: 136 Fat: 14g Carb: 30g Phosphorus: 50mg Potassium: 356mg Sodium: 71mg Protein: g

Chicken and Mandarin Salad

Preparation time: 40 minutes

Cooking time: 30 minutes

Servings: 3

Ingredients:

- 1 ½ - cup Chicken
- ½ - cup Celery
- ½ - cup Green pepper
- ¼ - cup Onion, finely sliced
- ¼ - cup Light mayonnaise
- ½ - tsp. freshly ground pepper

Directions:

1. Hurl chicken, celery, green pepper and onion to blend. Include mayo and pepper. Blend delicately and serve.

Nutrition: Calories 375, Fat 15, Fiber 2, Carbs 14, Protein 28

Soup & Stews

Delicious Tomato Basil Soup

Preparation Time: 10 minutes

Cooking Time: 20 minutes

Servings: 6

Ingredients:

- 28 oz. can tomato, diced
- 1 1/2 cups chicken stock
- 1/2 tsp Italian seasoning
- 1/2 tsp garlic, minced
- 1 onion, chopped
- 1/4 cup fresh basil leaves
- 1/2 cup heavy cream
- 2 tbsp. butter
- Pepper
- Salt

Directions:

1. Melt butter in a saucepan over medium-high heat.
2. Add onion and garlic sauté for 5 minutes.
3. Add Red bell peppers, Italian seasoning, and broth. Stir well and bring to boil over high heat.
4. Turn heat to medium-low and simmer for 8-10 minutes.
5. Blend the soup using an immersion blender until smooth.
6. Add heavy cream and basil and stir well. Season soup with pepper and salt.

7. Stir and serve.

Nutrition: Calories 108 Fat 7.8 g Carbohydrates 9.1 g Sugar 5.5 g Protein 1.9 g Cholesterol 24 mg Phosphorus: 110mg Potassium: 137mg Sodium: 95mg

Shredded Pork Soup

Preparation Time: 10 minutes

Cooking Time: 8 hours

Servings: 8

Ingredients:

- 1 lb. pork loin
- 8 cups chicken broth
- 2 tsp fresh lime juice
- 1 1/2 tsp garlic powder
- 1 1/2 tsp onion powder
- 1 1/2 tsp chili powder
- 1 1/2 tsp cumin
- 1 jalapeno pepper, minced
- 1 cup onion, chopped
- 3 Red bell peppers, chopped

Directions:

1. Add Red bell peppers, jalapeno, and onion into the slow cooker and stir well.
2. Place meat on top of the tomato mixture.
3. Pour remaining ingredients on top of the meat.
4. Cover slow cooker and cook on low for 8 hours.
5. Remove meat from slow cooker and shred using a fork.
6. Return shredded meat to the slow cooker and stir well.
7. Serve and enjoy.

Nutrition: Calories 199 Fat 9.6 g Carbohydrates 6.3 g Sugar 3.1 g Protein 21.2 g Cholesterol 45 mg Phosphorus: 140mg Potassium: 127mg Sodium: 95mg

Curried Carrot and Beet Soup

Preparation Time: 10 minutes

Cooking Time: 50 minutes

Servings: 4

Ingredients:

- large red beet
- 5 carrots, chopped
- 1 tablespoon curry powder
- cups Homemade Rice Almond milk or unsweetened store-bought rice almond milk
- Freshly ground black pepper
- Yogurt, for serving

Directions:

1. Preheat the oven to 400°F.
2. Wrap the beet in aluminum foil and roast for 45 minutes, until the vegetable is tender when pierced with a fork. Remove from the oven and let cool.
3. Add the carrots and cover with water. Bring to a boil, reduce the heat, cover, and simmer for 10 minutes, until tender.
4. Transfer the carrots and beet to a food processor, and process until smooth. Add the curry powder and rice almond milk. Season with pepper. Serve topped with a dollop of yogurt.

5. Substitution tip: Carrots are high in potassium. If you need to reduce your potassium further, use 2 carrots instead of 5. The soup will be a little thinner but still have a carrot flavor and just 322mg of potassium.

Nutrition: Calories: 112; Total Fat: 1g; Saturated Fat: 0g; Cholesterol: 0mg; Carbohydrates: 24g; Fiber: 7g; Protein: 3g; Phosphorus: 57mg; Potassium: 468mg; Sodium: 129mg

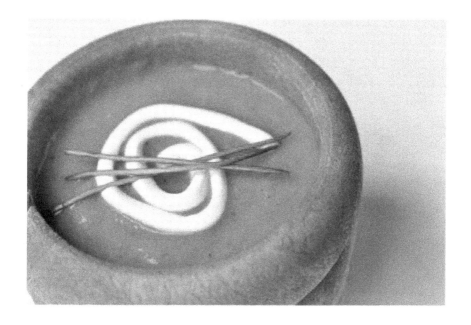

Cauliflower Soup

Preparation Time: 15 minutes

Cooking Time: 10 minutes

Servings: 4

Ingredients:

- Unsalted butter – 1 tsp.
- Sweet onion – 1 small, chopped
- Minced garlic – 2 tsps.
- Small head cauliflower – 1, cut into small florets
- Curry powder – 2 tsps.
- Water to cover the cauliflower
- Light sour cream – ½ cup
- Chopped fresh cilantro – 3 Tbsps.

Directions:

1. Heat the butter over a medium-high heat and sauté the onion-garlic for about 3 minutes or until softened.
2. Add the cauliflower, water, and curry powder.
3. Bring the soup to a simmer, then decrease the heat to low and simmer for 20 minutes or until the cauliflower is tender.
4. Puree the soup until creamy and smooth with a hand mixer.
5. Transfer the soup back into a saucepan and stir in the sour cream and cilantro.

6. Heat the soup on medium heat for 5 minutes or until warmed through.

Nutrition: Calories: 33 Fat: 2g Carb: 4g Phosphorus: 30mg Potassium: 167mg Sodium: 22mg Protein: 1g

Cabbage Stew

Preparation Time: 20 minutes

Cooking Time: 35 minutes

Servings: 6

Ingredients:

- Unsalted butter – 1 tsp.
- Large sweet onion - ½, chopped
- Minced garlic – 1 tsp.
- Shredded green cabbage – 6 cups
- Celery stalks - 3, chopped with leafy tops
- Scallion – 1, both green and white parts, chopped
- Chopped fresh parsley – 2 Tbsps.
- Freshly squeezed lemon juice – 2 Tbsps.
- Chopped fresh thyme – 1 Tbsp.
- Chopped savory – 1 tsp.
- Chopped fresh oregano – 1 tsp.
- Water
- Fresh green beans – 1 cup, cut into 1-inch pieces
- Ground black pepper

Directions:

1. Melt the butter in a pot.
2. Sauté the onion and garlic in the melted butter for 3 minutes, or until the vegetables are softened.

3. Add the celery, cabbage, scallion, parsley, lemon juice, thyme, savory, and oregano to the pot, add enough water to cover the vegetables by 4 inches.
4. Bring the soup to a boil. Reduce the heat to low and simmer the soup for 25 minutes or until the vegetables are tender.
5. Season with pepper.

Nutrition: Calories: 33 Fat: 1g Carb: 6g Phosphorus: 29mg Potassium: 187mg Sodium: 20mg Protein: 1g

Creamy Vinaigrette

Preparation time: 15 minutes

Cooking time: 25 minutes

Servings: 4

Ingredients:

- 2 - tbsp. cider vinegar
- 2 - tbsp. lime or lemon juice
- 1 - Garlic clove, minced
- 1 - tsp. Dijon mustard
- 1 - tsp. ground cumin
- ½ - cup sour cream
- 2 - tbsp. olive oil
- ¼ - tsp. black pepper

Directions:

1. Consolidate all fixings and blend well. Fill serving of mixed greens carafe. Chill.

Nutrition: Calories 188, Fat 15, Fiber 8, Carbs 35, Protein 25

Dessert

Lemony Blackberry Granita

Preparation time: 15 minutes

Cooking time: 0 minutes

Servings: 4

Ingredients:

- 1 pound (454 g) fresh blackberries
- 1 teaspoon chopped fresh thyme
- ¼ cup freshly squeezed lemon juice
- ½ cup raw honey
- ½ cup water

Directions:

1. Put all the ingredients in a food processor, then pulse to purée. Pour the mixture through a sieve into a baking dish. Discard the seeds remain in the sieve.
2. Put the baking dish in the freezer for 2 hours. Remove the dish from the refrigerator and stir to break any frozen parts.
3. Return the dish back to the freezer for an hour, then stir to break any frozen parts again. Return the dish to the freezer for 4 hours until the granita is completely frozen.
4. Remove it from the freezer and mash to serve.

Nutrition: calories: 183 fat: 1.1g protein: 2.2g carbs: 45.9g

Cucumber sandwich Bites

Preparation Time: 5 minutes

Cooking Time: 0 minutes

Servings: 12

Ingredients:

- 1 cucumber, sliced
- 8 slices whole wheat bread
- 2 tablespoons cream cheese, soft
- 1 tablespoon chives, chopped
- ¼ cup avocado, peeled, pitted and mashed
- 1 teaspoon mustard
- Salt and black pepper to the taste

Directions:

1. Spread the mashed avocado on each bread slice, also spread the rest of the ingredients except the cucumber slices.
2. Divide the cucumber slices on the bread slices, cut each slice in thirds, arrange on a platter and serve as an appetizer.

Nutrition: calories 187 fat 12.4g carbohydrates 4.5g Protein 8.2g

Yogurt Dip

Preparation Time: 10 minutes

Cooking Time: 0 minutes

Servings: 6

Ingredients:

- 2 cups greek yogurt
- 2 tablespoons pistachios, toasted and chopped
- A pinch of salt and white pepper
- 2 tablespoons mint, chopped
- 1 tablespoon kalamata olives, pitted and chopped
- ¼ cup zaatar spice
- ¼ cup pomegranate seeds
- 1/3 cup olive oil

Directions:

1. Mix the yogurt with the pistachios and the rest of the ingredients, whisk well, divide into small cups and serve with pita chips on the side.

Nutrition: calories 294 fat 18g carbohydrates 2g protein 10g

Tomato Bruschetta

Preparation Time: 10 minutes

Cooking Time: 10 minutes

Servings: 6

Ingredients:

- 1 baguette, sliced
- 1/3 cup basil, chopped
- 6 tomatoes, cubed
- 2 garlic cloves, minced
- A pinch of salt and black pepper
- 1 teaspoon olive oil
- 1 tablespoon balsamic vinegar
- ½ teaspoon garlic powder
- Cooking spray

Directions:

1. Situate the baguette slices on a baking sheet lined with parchment paper, grease with cooking spray. Bake for 10 minutes at 400 degrees.
2. Combine the tomatoes with the basil and the remaining ingredients, toss well and leave aside for 10 minutes. Divide the tomato mix on each baguette slice, arrange them all on a platter and serve.

Nutrition: calories 162 fat 4g carbohydrates 29g protein 4g

Olives and Cheese Stuffed Tomatoes

Preparation Time: 10 minutes

Cooking Time: 0 minutes

Servings: 24

Ingredients:

- 24 cherry tomatoes, top cut off and insides scooped out
- 2 tablespoons olive oil
- ¼ teaspoon red pepper flakes
- ½ cup feta cheese, crumbled
- 2 tablespoons black olive paste
- ¼ cup mint, torn

Directions:

1. In a bowl, mix the olives paste with the rest of the ingredients except the cherry tomatoes and whisk well. Stuff the cherry tomatoes with this mix, arrange them all on a platter and serve as an appetizer.

Nutrition: calories 136 fat 8.6g carbohydrates 5.6g protein 5.1g

Thank you!